THE
PATH
Forward

THE
PATH
Forward

MYRA WOODBRIDGE

Inquiries and Book Orders should be addressed to:

WRITER'S TORCH
Press & Media

Writer's Torch Press & Media
Email: admin@writerstorch.com
Phone: 347-768-7550

Printed in the United States of America

ISBN: 979-8-89175-123-1 (sc)
ISBN: 979-8-89175-124-8 (hc)

DEDICATION

I want to honor my husband, Terry, by dedicating this book to him. His strength and strong faith in the Lord have been a stalwart rampart for me throughout our life together.

All Glory and Honor remains with the Father, the Son, and the Holy Spirit.

PREFACE

The book you are now reading is a result of much joy and some agony. Sounds like life, doesn't it. Everyone's journey includes a little of this and a little of that. Sometimes, though, the negative can outweigh the positive, and it can be extremely hard to bear. We need help when it overtakes us. Perhaps you feel that way today or know someone who is experiencing that terrible sense of loss and heartache. The pain can be deep. At such times, we tend to ask ourselves "what did I do wrong?", or "is God angry with me?" and "I feel like I have failed the Lord". There are some who have been told "you brought it on yourself!". I think poor self-reflection comes to us all at times. But it isn't always the reality. It was planted there and my experience will show you how it can happen.

I do not have all the answers. I just know the One who does. That is why I wrote this book. I want you to see how no matter how devoted you are to the Lord, no matter how educated you are or how successful you are at your career – we all can face hard places that challenge our faith as we never dreamed possible! It can challenge what we know about *ourselves* too.

It is my hope that my testimony of the depth of love our Heavenly Father has for each of us, and to the extravagant

grace of God that is sufficient to redeem *every* failure –
whether real or imagined – will speak to your heart. It will
also show the awesome power of God that is more than
sufficient to raise us up from the dark places of our mind to
once again have clarity of self and purpose.

My story is not just about the downside of life. My
husband Terry and I faced a low point, but the Lord did
not leave us comfortless. He did not leave us in despair.
He is much better than that! He is much bigger than that!
Oh, He came to our rescue and gave us hope beyond our
disappointments and provided healing to the hurt in our
lives when we opened our hearts to His grace. Mending
broken vessels is His specialty, even when the vessel thinks
it is hopeless. It is not. It happens when _we_ make the right
choice to see that come about. That calls for obedience on
our part to do things His way. The healing that I longed for
would begin when I took that first step to do what I did not
think I could do! It was challenging to my flesh, yes. But, it
was very much worth it. I rejoiced afterwards and I'm still
thankful that the Lord strengthened me to take that step. It
was my turning point.

I will also share with you the lessons I learned from this
challenging place we walked through. Every battle has its
victory, and one aspect of that victory is the wisdom and
the knowledge we gain. God really did turn pain into gain!
There is a verse in the Book of Isiah that describes the way
the Lord ministered to our lives. It is found in chapter 61: 3.
In this verse, Isaiah wrote of the Anointed One that would
come and He would appoint those that mourn in Zion,
to give them beauty for ashes, the oil of joy for mourning,

the garment of praise for the spirit of heaviness; that they may be called trees of righteousness, the planting of the Lord, that He may be glorified". NKJV. I checked the word "appoint" in the Hebrew concordance. Some versions use the word "console". The meaning includes: *to be firm, to settle.* I considered that and I believe this text provides the promise that the Lord Jesus, who is the Anointed One that Israel had been waiting for, would have a multi-faceted ministry.

It would include Him wanting to be there for us in our most challenging life experiences and give us His peace, and His comfort which enables us to be settled in our mind, in our spirit from all the noise about us, from all the turmoil *within* us, and to be "grounded" in Him and in His Word in a greater way. He can provide that stability to our hearts so that we will not be moved from our faith in Him by *any* circumstance of life we face, *even* if and when it is demonically inspired. One more thing, in Luke 4: 16-21 the Lord Jesus stood in the Temple on a Sabbath day and read from Isaiah 61and boldly declared to those in attendance that He was the fulfillment of those words. These words are as relevant today as they were in that Temple. We can trust in the Anointed One to bring them to pass in our lives.

Our journey would teach us that at each turn, on every mountain, in every valley, at any crossroads we came to, we could take His hand, listen to His voice, and get in step with Him on The Path Forward, following His lead. The Light of His Word would shine the way before us.

"Your Word is a lamp unto my feet, and a
light unto my path." Psalm 119:105

CONTENTS

CHAPTER ONE

One Step at a Time

Terry and I were married on a beautiful day in May, although, it started out cloudy! About 3 hours before the wedding, I stepped outside my hotel room where my maid of honor and I were getting all dolled up for the ceremony. I looked at those skies and I really didn't want it to rain on the wedding party or the guests coming. I looked up to the sky and asked the Lord to please move the clouds out and not let it rain on our wedding day. It was a simple prayer from the heart of a bride. You know He answered! He gave us a glorious day to start our new life together. We would witness many more answers big and small and in between throughout our marriage.

From that point on, the Lord began to orchestrate circumstances that would build on each other a foundation of serving Him. Just two weeks after we married, we "just happened" to find the church that would strengthen us in our knowledge of the Lord and His Word. From that, God began to use is in small ways, just to get our "feet wet" in serving Him. The word "no" was not in our vocabulary in this regard. It always seemed the right thing to do. God was leading us along the Path He started for us. We assisted teachers in pre-teen classes and then in teen classes. This was really hands on training that provided good experience to build on. Several months later, I began sharing devotionals at a ladies prayer group. I did not have a job at that time so I had mornings free. I would use that time to study our Finnis J. Dake Bible each day till noon. Terry had his quiet time of study much earlier in the morning. God was building a foundation of truth in our lives. He continues to solidify that. We never outgrow the need to study the Scripture. Now, we have two commentaries we can review and six study Bibles that we are confident in.

Through the years, God has blessed to use us in some capacity in and out of the church community. Terry served as a chaplain in a professional organization that related to his job. We had a weekly radio program for years and one that was a daily five minute inspirational program that was on early in the morning so commuters could listen. I have always taught an adult class for Sunday mornings wherever we were, and Terry has always been in church leadership. We have cleaned the church and we have fed the church. And it has been our privilege to do so. We wouldn't change a thing.

In 2002 we had a Sunday morning class at Mount Holly Church in Carrollton, Georgia. It was a wonderful class of people! They loved the Lord and loved His Word. We also held services on Monday nights in another town. We both sensed a stirring in our hearts to do something more for Him. Our vision wasn't complicated. It wasn't grandiose. It was a vision to see lives changed, people's needs met and to honor the Lord as He deserves in a different way than we had known. We sensed we were in a new season, and we were determined to wait on the Lord until we saw His hand orchestrating this new way for us.

We did not want to run ahead of Him, nor seek man's intervention. It was our responsibility to pray in faith for clear direction and to wait in faith. We were in a holding pattern. We soon came to understand that it takes just as much faith to hold steady as it does to step out! *Now* was not the time to make an untimely misstep or to give up on praying! To wait is not the same as doing nothing. To wait on the Lord is a hopeful anticipation of Him manifesting in our lives the very thing for which we have believed. It would be worth the wait!

Each prayer we pray *always* has a "Due Time" to be answered. Our hearts may say, "now, please!" But the wisdom of God determines otherwise. The Apostle Paul wrote in Galatians 6: 9 "And let us not be weary in well doing: for in due season we shall reap, if we faint not." There is a harvest of answers *on schedule* coming our way, as long as we do not rush ahead and make answers come about in our own strength. We came to realize that God had a purpose in our waiting for Him to answer our prayers. One reason for our wait was to *prepare* us for the answer! No time is wasted when you are on God's timeclock.

We also used this time to seek guidance from people we trust, those who have a strong prayer life, who have wisdom and have walked a similar path as we were walking at that time. We were always encouraged when we did so. One example of this was when we attended a Sunday morning service at Brownsville Assembly of God in Pensacola, Florida. Rev. John Kilpatrick was the pastor at that time. The revival that had been going on there for years was well known. On this beautiful spring morning, we would experience it firsthand. It was our twenty-ninth wedding anniversary, which made the day even more special. We were not disappointed in any way. There was a holy reverence that was immediately noticeable when we entered the church. We knew we were in the holy Presence of God. Just sensing the Lord's holiness kept me in tears for much of the service. It was both a humbling and a rewarding experience.

During the service, the Pastor opened the altar for anyone who desired prayer. The church's intercessory prayer team was assembled to pray with anyone individually. I remained seated while Terry went down for prayer concerning his ministry. One of the members of the intercessory prayer team earnestly prayed with him. When we left the service that day, we were more confident than ever that we were moving in the right direction through the assurance the Lord had placed within our hearts. Such assurance gives a person an inner peace that will sustain you through the days of waiting for the answer you have longed for to arrive.

Jesus has given us a promise to hold onto. It is found in Matthew 7: 7-8 "Ask, and it shall be given unto you; seek, and you shall find; knock, and it shall be opened unto you: For everyone that asks receives; and he that seeks finds; and to him that knocks it shall be opened." Occasionally, the Lord will answer with a "suddenly" where the door swings open and there it is! The answer you had been waiting for is right in front of you. You just walk on through, rejoicing.

Other times, it is a set time or a gradual time that the answer arrives. Either way…it is always ON time as far as God is concerned. We knew the Lord had us in a holding pattern. He would not fail to respond to our heart's cry for something more in our walk with Him. It could be around the corner!

After several weeks of praying together and with others, we felt it was time to take that first step of faith to see our vision come about. It actually felt more like a leap the morning we resigned from the church and the wonderful Sunday morning class that we loved. We carried each one in our hearts in the days that followed. If we want something more, we must be willing to let go of what we have always known! We were at peace knowing that God always has a good plan for His children as Jeremiah 29: 11 tells us: "For I know the thoughts that I think toward you, says the Lord, thoughts of peace and not of evil, to give you a future and a hope."

His plan *unfolds*; He doesn't give the big picture because the big picture could overwhelm us if we saw ALL that was ahead of us. As we continued our steps of faith, the more He revealed to us in time.

We did not expect a journey without difficulties. Regardless of how we serve the Lord, in a secular environment or in ministry, problems will arise. The reason for that is simple. People are people wherever we go. And we all fail, we hurt one another, we disappoint one another, we listen to the wrong voice at times and conflict arises. Often things happen when we least expect it. Things that you have no answers for! We may have been blindsided but God was not.

He would let us know: He was there all the time. Our future was in His hands.

> *"I will never leave you nor forsake you."*
> *Hebrews 13:6b*

CHAPTER TWO

While Waiting...
Keep Trusting

Leaving the known for the unknown is never easy. But it is worth it if we do not falter in our trust in God that He has us in the palm of His hand. There is no "hurry" in God. His wisdom knows the exact moment that He needs to step in, to initiate a plan, to bring about an answer, to conclude a matter. He wants us to trust in that wisdom because He always has our best interests at heart. He wants us to keep still in our spirit, resting in His sovereignty to change our position of "waiting" to "moving forward" when He directs us to do so.

As we waited, God had a few lessons He had in mind for us to learn. One of the lessons I learned was to be in the center of God's will, I would have to surrender mine. I hope this resonates with you as deeply as my experience was. His will is about Him, His purpose, His Kingdom, His way. Surrender is not easy. It costs us our comfort zone and our self-will. But it is the most rewarding life there is. It's a *daily* 24/7 choosing Him. The Gospel of Luke in chapter 14: 26-35, gives us the words of Jesus where He describes the person that can be His disciple. Here are the verses 26-27: "If any man come to Me, and hate not his father; and mother; and wife, and children, and brethren, and sisters, yea, and his own life also, he cannot be my disciple. And whosoever does not bear his cross, and come after me, cannot be my disciple." That is very strong isn't it! It isn't about us having animosity toward any person, especially our own family. It is about not loving others less but *loving Him more* than anyone in our lives – including ourselves. Jesus does not accept second place in anyone's life. He calls for a total commitment to His will, to His purpose, to His Kingdom, to His way. After all, He is worthy of this kind of complete devotion.

To be sure, when a person determines to seek the Lord to direct you in His will, there will be a battle to come about. It will be a spiritual conflict where the enemy of our soul, satan himself, will set up roadblocks in our seeing that manifest in our lives. We were not an exception to this rule. As Terry and I remained in our holding pattern, the enemy sought to war against our mind about it, trying to make us impatient, to make us disappointed, to make us give up on God, and to think that God had "let us down". Of course, that wasn't true – and never could be – but we have to remember: satan does not tell the truth.

This is how he operates. He seeks to wear us down, defeat us, weaken us, harass us – all with one aim: destroy our faith in Christ and His Word. That is at the heart of every battle that the enemy sets up against us. Our faith is the target. And he works against our most vulnerable area: our flesh – because our flesh is so weak!

Jesus warned His disciples of this in the Garden of Gethsemane, when He told those He found sleeping while He was praying: "Watch and pray, lest you enter into temptation. The spirit indeed is willing, but the flesh is weak." The enemy knows our weak areas and he will try every trick in the book to deter us from God's plan for our lives. God's plan is His Word. The enemy doesn't care if we attend every church service and every Bible study and every prayer meeting! He just doesn't want us to put our faith in the Scripture and apply it to our lives. Because the Word gets results in our lives!

You might ask – how do we apply the Word of God to our lives? First, if there is any truth in this world, it is found in this sacred Book. It is not only about do's and don'ts. We can consider it a manual to guide us in making the best choices for our lives. We have learned to ask the Lord in prayer for the verse we need to stand upon for the current situation we are facing. When we pray, His Spirit will impress upon our heart the verse or an instructive direction that will apply to the challenge. It is up to us then to walk it out. The Lord has been faithful to help us in this way! In 1987 I had a serious health issue come about. I saw more than one doctor and had several tests done. I eventually was diagnosed with a form of cancer in the bronchial tube. Each time I had to see a doctor, I would ask the Lord for a Scripture. He would give me a verse or passage. Each time we were encouraged by that Word, which gave us strength to face the unknown – and even the known. I am alive today because His Word came true in my health and because Terry prayed – and many others also prayed – I'm still around to declare God's goodness to those who will hear. That is how we apply Scripture to our lives today. When we pray and sincerely ask the Lord to direct us and we wait for Him to do so, He will lead us. When He does, then we walk it out, we essentially come into agreement with the word God gives us and determine to make our choices accordingly. Victory will come.

Several years ago, we really needed to get a new car for me to drive to work and for general purposes. We looked for a while and finally found a used 1985 Thunderbird, black with gray interior. We went through the sales routine and could not come to terms. It gave me a splitting headache! We left without buying the car. We agreed to pray and hear from the Lord on whether to go back and come to terms or look elsewhere. We did just that. Let me say….when you pray, you ask in faith and you ask in sincerity - you ask with the mindset that you will *accept* however the Lord directs you. That isn't always the easiest thing to do! It wasn't that morning when we prayed about the 1985 Thunderbird. Terry prayed, I prayed. I was ready to buy it because I was willing to accept that car to be the one for us. I was being led by my *need* and not by wisdom. After Terry prayed, he told me he did not feel that the Lord wanted us to buy the car. I was so disappointed. He was too. But we determined to make the purchase only if and when it was the right one. I needed a new car. Terry knew that. The Lord knew that! But it wasn't *that* car that I needed as I would soon discover. Too often we go by what *appears* to be our answer when God has the *real* answer down the road. It was a case of fact vs fiction, patience vs desperation.

I had more than one choice to make that day. Would I trust the Lord to speak to my husband and would I trust Terry to listen as he had done in the past or would I let my need supersede the path of wisdom. I determined to trust the Lord to lead Terry and I would agree with it because we are a team. A team pulls together, never against each other. Regardless. Yes, I wanted the car. But I wanted to stay on the right path more. I determined to say yes but my flesh was not happy! We both had to submit our own desires to the Lord and wait for Him to lead us to the right vehicle. It wasn't too long after this that we went to a different dealership to look around. We found our answer! The Lord worked it out so wonderfully because He blessed us to buy a new 1986 Thunderbird, black with gray interior and all the bells and whistles that we wanted! The Lord gave us something much better after we made choices that were in line with His Word and His will and His way. The Lord did this time and again throughout our lives.

It is, of course, our mind where all our choices are made. At times the choices can be very challenging, hard to bear, much more significant than buying a car. But if we learn to pray about our choices, pray about our needs, pray about our circumstances and wait to hear what God says about them, then we *set the pattern* in our lives that this is how we are going to handle life: prayer + God's Word + God's leading. This is incredibly important when we find ourselves facing spiritual conflict because it is in our mind where the war takes place. We can vacillate between what I want vs what is totally wrong vs what is best. The Lord in His great wisdom has provided the means for us to overcome the mental conflict and have clarity in how to move forward. Day in, day out. It centers on His Word.

Paul the apostle gives us the answer in Ephesians 6:10-18 where he details the believer's spiritual armor to face any spiritual struggle we have and come out of it in victory. I want to give special attention to one verse in particular. It is verse 17 where he wrote: "And take the helmet of salvation, and the sword of the Spirit, which is the Word of God". When anyone wears a helmet, it lets all those who see it know which team they play for in sports or which branch of military they serve or in law enforcement. They think in terms of who they are and what they do in life in that role. That role gives them guidelines to carry out their job and direction on its application.

Our helmet of salvation defines us as a member of the Lord's army. We are His. We have been bought with a price for which He paid at Calvary. We serve King Jesus and He doesn't lose battles. The helmet covers our mind, reminding us who we are *in Christ*, why we are here on this earth and where we are going someday. Our thoughts need to line up with these basic truths and reject thoughts of doubt, thereby *renewing our mind* and enabling us to win our battles. No team, nor any branch of the military ever wins if they forget they are on a winning team, headed up by a superior leader.

"The Sword of the Spirit, which is the Word of God" gives us our offensive weapon. The Greek word for sword speaks to a short sword or dagger, perhaps no more than 14 inches long. A soldier would use such a weapon in hand-to-hand combat. This lets us know, the enemy will try to get as close as he possibly can to intimidate us and take us down. We, in our own strength, are no match for him and the hosts that serve him. BUT… the good news is: Jesus did that for us at Calvary and His blood covers us and His Word is available for us to speak forth against our attacker. The Greek term that is used for "word" in verse 17 is rhema, which is defined as a specific word from the Bible for the circumstance we are facing or the Holy Spirit may give us instructions to follow – which is always in line with the Scripture. That is the very thing that will prevail against our enemy. It works. It worked for me and it will work for anyone who believes it and applies it to their life.

There were many days absolutely nothing changed for us. But, a walk of faith is exactly that at times! We do not understand when we cannot see with our natural eyes how God is working in our behalf. That is when we had to *just keep trusting*. Proverbs 4: 26-27 tells us "Ponder the path of thy feet and let all thy ways be established. Turn not to the right hand nor to the left: remove thy foot from evil." I suppose one of the hardest things for us humans to do is to "wait". Our faith is being tested during our "wait" time. He wants to see if we are going to take matters into our own hands or wait on His perfect plan. This can only mean we lay down our will at the foot of the cross and wait for His plan to manifest in our lives.

Yes! God would eventually align circumstances and people in our lives for His purpose. First, His plan would include teaching us about walking out His will in such a way we would never forget the secrets learned. One step at a time.

"Order my steps in Your word"
Psalm 119: 133a

CHAPTER THREE

Change? ME Change??

Change happens in life but usually no one likes it very much. We typically see no need to personally change while we easily see the need for *others* to change. But positive change benefits everyone and it has the power to affect all areas of our lives – home, work, church – all our relationships.

If there is just one word that would define what becoming a Christian is all about is this: transformation. This is change from the inside out. When Jesus came to this earth, He came with a mandate from His Father – be the One that provides *change* to any person who believes in Him as His only begotten Son, and trusts in Him as their Savior through His death on the cross for the sins of the world. Life *can* be different and this is the starting point for any of us.

When we take that step of faith to trust in Christ, a magnificent *change* takes place deep within our soul. The Scripture speaks of it as becoming a "new creation". I'll give you the entire verse from II Corinthians 5: 17 which says: "Therefore, if anyone is in Christ, he is a new creation; old things have passed away; behold, all things have become new."

Our new life in Christ does not mean we no longer need to experience change. Far from it. Our new birth experience is only the beginning of the transformational process of the new person God has destined each believer to be. He has in mind our becoming more like His Son. Scripture tells us about this in Romans 8: 29: "For whom He foreknew, He also predestined to be conformed to the image of His Son, that He might be the firstborn among many brethren." That sounds like *change* is on God's agenda for us all.

This is the goodness of God continuing in our lives after our new birth experience! He loves us so much that He doesn't want us to remain the same as we were. He wants to develop in us the image of His dear Son, the wholly perfect One. This does not happen quickly. And it certainly calls for change. It is a lifetime project that God is determined to see to completion. Philippians 1: 6 speaks to this: "being confident of this very thing, that He who has begun a good work in you will complete it until the day of Jesus Christ." Yes, what God starts, He finishes.

I'm very thankful that the Lord is so patient that despite our imperfections – His will for our lives remains intact. The story of the Potter and his work on a clay vessel from Jeremiah 18 comes to mind. In verse 2, the Lord speaks to the prophet to go down to the potter's house where He would cause Jeremiah to hear His words. As I understand from Dake's Study Bible, there was a clay field south of Jerusalem beyond the valley of Hinnom. It was in this location that the potters could work their craft. Inside the potter's house, there was an instrument that had 2 wheels, the lower one was worked by the feet to give motion to the upper one that was a flat disc or plate of wood. It was on this plate that he would lay the clay to be molded by his hands.

This work of clay did not happen by accident. It was intentional, and precise, with the potter always mindful that his hands were stronger than the clay and must be formed with care as the wheel would revolve quickly. This could not be performed by an amateur. It is solely the work of a master potter.

Jeremiah 18 tells us that Jeremiah did as the Lord asked and as he entered the potter's house, he sees the artisan at work with the clay on the wheel. Then Verse 4 happens. It says: "And the vessel that he made of clay was marred in the hand of the potter: so he made it again another vessel, as seemed good to the potter to make it."

The potter is amazing. He found imperfection in the clay that may have been resistant to the working hands of the potter. *Yet, he did not throw the clay away.* He never became frustrated, giving up on the clay. He knew exactly what to do. Confront the area of resistance, taking as much time as was needed to make the necessary *change*. He did so with grace and patience. He removed the hindrance and continued his work with it. His design for the vessel would prevail. It would become useful because he saw in it what others did not.

I want *you* to think about this entire paragraph and especially the last sentence. Regardless of your life circumstance, God still sees value in you. He still has a purpose for your life. Don't listen to the lie of satan. God has not given up on you SO don't you give up on Him! Turn to Him and pour your heart out to Him.

Every Christian will experience their turn on the Potter's wheel. It is the first step – but not the last one – toward becoming the vessel the Lord always had in mind for each of us to be. The primary purpose: to reflect the image of His Son.

In retrospect, Terry and I can see how the Lord used our time of waiting for His new assignment for us to "nudge" us in areas that needed attention. He continues to nudge us still, and we are thankful that His mercy endures forever, and He keeps working with us – all believers – for that singular purpose of seeing more of Jesus in our lives. This is always obvious in our response to others, in showing God's love to those that seem unconcerned for us, extending mercy when others offend us, our willingness to forgive even if the offender never asks us to do so, our kindness to all, not showing partiality, extending generosity, being faithful to our commitments, losing a critical attitude.

The apostle Peter had his challenges – just like you and me. He could be impatient, quick tempered, abrasive, say things he lived to regret. He even took a sword and cut off the ear of one of the soldiers that came to arrest the Lord the night He was betrayed. Jesus rebuked him for that and healed the soldier's ear. Yes! Jesus cared enough to do good to one of those soldiers whose only interest was arresting the Healer. John18: 10-11. This kind of love in action and this kind of mercy doesn't come naturally! It comes from the Holy Spirit pouring it in our hearts as we submit our hard heartedness to Him. This may take a lifetime but its impact is far reaching.

This same Peter experienced a dramatic change. The Book of Acts contains many occasions where he was used to pray and healings and salvations took place. The Potter was able to accomplish the necessary transformation in his heart so that others could experience the goodness of God at work in their lives.

The highest attribute a Christian can have is a servant's heart. Yes, change me, Lord. To be sure: nothing changes in those areas we want to see changed *for us* unless we say yes to the changes God determines *in us*.

> *"Let love be without hypocrisy. Abhor what is evil.*
> *Cling to what is good. Be kindly affectionate to*
> *one another with brotherly love, in honor giving*
> *preference to one another; not lagging in diligence,*
> *fervent in spirit, serving the Lord" Romans 12: 9-11*

CHAPTER FOUR

The Door Opens

While we were thankful that the Lord was preparing us for the future, our present status remained the same. We still seemed to be in a spiritual holding pattern. To avoid making a decision that could be disastrous we decided to ask close friends to come together again to seek the Lord and ask Him to confirm we were on the right track or that we had made a colossal error in leaving our church home and teaching ministry there. We needed answers. We needed the Lord to speak to our hearts in such a way that would give us clear direction.

When you set your heart to seek the Lord, He will not disappoint. As a result of our coming together to pray, God refreshed our spirit and renewed our hope that His answer was on the way! We did not know "HOW" but we did know "WHO" would walk us through this uncharted territory for us. He confirmed to our hearts that it was time to begin having church services in our home. This would provide opportunity to determine if the services were meant to be short or long term. It was a way to "test the waters". There was no need for a public venue at this early stage. Wisdom called for a solid financial structure before moving to a public arena.

We began to tell people what our plans were and invited them to be with us. We trusted the Lord to bring the people to the services who He wanted to be a part of this new work. It would be people who wanted something more. Slowly but surely, we were seeing the Lord open this new door of ministry. We were thrilled to be on the brink of a new opportunity to serve the Lord and advance His Kingdom.

Whatever you do in life, whatever worthy goal you set, your top priority should always be to cover it in prayer. God can bring things about that will leave no doubt that He orchestrated it. You may have been waiting a long time. That's OK. Continue to pray. Keep your eyes on the Lord and listen for His voice to lead you. He will always lead us in the way of peace.

If you make a decision that is out of His will for your life, you will not have peace about it. The absence of peace is the absence of the right direction. STOP and ask Him for the answer that will lead you in the way of peace. Colossians 3: 15 speaks to us in this regard: "And let the peace of God rule in your hearts, to which also you were called in one body; and be thankful." Here the apostle Paul was telling the church to let peace act as an umpire in our hearts, deciding when we are on the right track or if we are missing it all together. No one wants to be called "out". Peace can guide us to make the best choices and keep our mind clear of doubt and worry and frustration. The enemy will hinder answers, can set up circumstances to make us think 'it just isn't going to happen for us', you might as well go back to square one! No, don't let satan move you from your position of faith because your faith is his target. I can't say this enough! Resist that. Pray again. Pray in faith, hope, love. Guard your heart by hiding the Word of God in your heart instead. That will strengthen you and enable you to continue to stand strong.

If you ever get sidetracked or off course, don't fear! Draw near to the Lord again and trust Him to right your ship! He will steer us in the way to make any changes that are necessary. Prayer is the most positive way of keeping our hearts sensitive to His leading. He leads those who are willing to follow. God doesn't force us. *He leads us*, which means we must keep our eyes upon Him to see *how* He leads.

> *"I will instruct you and teach you in the way you*
> *should go; I will guide you with My eye."*
> *Psalm 32: 8*

Chapter Five

God's Workmanship

There is a beautiful verse in Scripture in Ephesians 2: 10 that tells us: "For we are His workmanship, created in Christ Jesus for good works, which God prepared beforehand that we should walk in them." The Greek word for workmanship is *poiema*. (Emphasis on the "ie".) It sounds very much like our English word "poem". It refers to something created, designed, and built by a master craftsman, an artisan. This kind of workmanship takes time and talent and a keen eye for the process as the potter that I mentioned earlier in this book. This verse refers to God's sovereign Hands creating us for a special purpose in this life. A purpose where our God-given talents and abilities are best served, to benefit others, to affect the world for the sake of Christ and for His glory.

After we left Mount Holly, it really felt to Terry and I both like we had been sitting on the shelf after actively serving for many years. We were just waiting for the Master to reach up and say "Now, it is time, follow My lead." He had taken us from the Potters wheel to once again be useful in His Kingdom. We were so blessed to see God's plan for us unfold. We were at the beginning stage of seeing something more in our ministry.

To experience something more in our life, to see circumstances change, to see personal changes, demands we *do* something more, something beyond what we are presently doing, making different choices, listening to wiser voices, be willing to change our attitude and keep to it. And the big one – stop making excuses! It isn't what other people are doing or not doing – what are YOU doing to see positive change come about.

Springtime is my favorite time of the year. I so enjoy the beauty of nature that miraculously comes forth from something that looked so dead all winter! There are those in our community that plant gardens and flowers that are gorgeous. I could wish to have some in my own yard or make excuses as to why I don't. OR, I could decide to get out there and get things prepared so as to plant the flowers I want to grow. When I do, amazing beauty is in MY yard, not just in the neighbors. My point is obvious. God didn't plant the flowers for me. He blessed me to make the choice to do what was necessary to change how the yard looks around the house. And He blessed me to have Terry help me with it all! I get up every morning and look out and see beauty and it blesses me.

It all comes down to how much do we really want change and will we make that extra effort to receive it. Will we discipline ourselves, will we pray for it, will we turn our life over to Christ for Him to change us for it? The Lord wants to bless us! But not for us to remain the same. He blesses for us to become better! For us to grow as a human being and most of all, as a Christian! He is ever working on us as His workmanship.

I was in a doctor's office one day and the doctor had a portrait of his son and himself. The artist did a fabulous job on the portrait. I happened to notice something remarkable about the portrait though. As I stood there before the portrait, I saw the vast colors of different hues – all that the artist used to make one portrait. The artist seemed to capture the love the father had for his son and the pride, as well, and rightly so. I could see the love the son had for his dad too, the closeness the two enjoyed, how he looked up to his dad.

Then, I sat down over to the side of the room. I looked at the portrait again and I couldn't believe my eyes! From that perspective, I could actually see dark shadings in the portrait! Where did they come from? It was the handiwork of the same artist! I had to change my perspective to realize that the dark shadings were only a portion of the painting, not the whole and they were necessary to highlight the beauty of it all.

I was moved to tears thinking of how God gives us life and places within us great abilities to think and reason and love and care for others. We also have dark experiences come about but it doesn't mean they have to destroy us or make us hard-hearted. Hardness of the heart renders the person less usable.

The dark experiences can be overcome with God's help and made into something positive that adds to our life by learning from them, giving us depth of character and sensitivity to others. There is a beautiful verse in Romans 8: 28 – which is a favorite of countless believers. It says:

"And we know that all things work together for good to those who love God, to those who are the called according to His purpose." This verse alone confirms the beauty of the goodness of God in how He works in our lives. Yes, the reality of living in a fallen world is obvious every single day. There is a lot of negative to deal with, a lot of sorrow, a lot of heartache in this world. But God has a way of "working things together" to bring about something positive from it. The Greek word for "good" in this verse has to do with something beneficial. Sometimes, it may be an important lesson is learned that teaches us wisdom that we can take through the rest of our lives. At some point we will be able to share that wisdom with others.

God really is able to redeem any circumstance, any life, if we will but trust Him to do so. You don't believe me? There are so many examples of God doing this very thing in people's lives in the Scripture! Just consider the 11th chapter of Hebrews. This chapter not only defines faith in God, but it provides real life examples of people who did not just talk faith but actually walked it out. There are no saints on this list. They were human beings just like you and me. People who trusted God above their circumstance of life and put their hope in Him to "work" their circumstance into something positive. Faith will change our perspective in how we view things, even the bad things that happen, when we view them through the prism of God's Word and His goodness.

Paul the apostle wrote about a challenging experience he had in II Corinthians 1st chapter. He suffered greatly and at one point, he was concerned for his very life! Verses 3-4 tell us: "Blessed be the God and Father of our Lord Jesus Christ, the Father of mercies and God of all comfort, Who comforts us in all our tribulation, that we may be able to comfort those who are in any trouble, with the comfort with which we ourselves are comforted by God." Paul's perspective was, yes, it was a very difficult experience for me, and I was concerned for my life, but God intervened miraculously for me, and it has given me a testimony to share with others to encourage them to know how faithful the Lord is. He will be for them as well!

Yes, our challenges and our blessings are all a part of the portrait of our lives. The strokes of colors that blend and the underlying shadings that provide depth. That awful thing we are facing today can be a useful testimony to someone else one day and will help them on their journey.

We are all a work in progress. A work of art with many colors and variations. We are going from glory to glory as the Scripture tells us. "But we all, with unveiled face, beholding as in a mirror the glory of the Lord, are being transformed into the same image from glory to glory, just as by the Spirit of the Lord". II Corinthians 3: 18. The Lord is at work in each of our lives to develop that certain image that increases over time and will reflect His Son in our lives, making us a fine representative for Him. It will be worth it all!

The Lord allowed Terry and I to begin this journey and He would use us in ways and circumstances that we had never experienced before. When things started so well, we never gave it thought of the dark shadings that would come about as they did. I would learn just how important having the right perspective really is.

*"But we have this treasure in earthen
vessels, that the excellence of the power
may be of God and not of us."*
II Corinthians 4: 7

CHAPTER SIX

The Setup

It was a major step of faith for us to begin a church. We were not professionals! We were just willing to do it. We longed to see great things from the Lord. He gave us the desires of our heart and with it, the responsibility to hold His Name high. It was obvious that the Lord's Hand was orchestrating people to be involved in this work. We were so blessed to meet and come to hold dear the lovely people who chose to be a part of our ministry. Throughout our season of ministry as a church, we witnessed so many answers to prayer. It was a testament to the strength and power of unity in the faith and God's great goodness to answer prayer! Yet, with all the blessings, a certain amount of stress came too. Then a little became a lot.

As with any church, there is typically a nucleus of people who work closely with you in the essential areas of ministry. We relied on them and trusted their commitment to the church. Our hearts were knit together for the goal of serving Christ and lifting Him up. It was a joy to serve together. To be sure, none of us were perfect. We all had our imperfections and at different times and different circumstances – they were visible. But we loved each other and remained steadfast in our purpose. Until that purpose changed for some. It isn't that they were wrong, and we were right or vice versa. It simply means, people can change course without notice and people can get hurt, can be disappointed, disillusioned.

It isn't uncommon for people to leave a church. It can happen for a myriad of reasons. Some are justified, some are not. Since we were a young church, everyone was aware of their absence. The congregation felt like a family, so it was a definite disappointment to us all. But we needed to continue to serve and lead as the Lord would have us to.

Tension only increased for me. I was already having a lot of anxiety, while carrying a lot of weight on my shoulders *that I took on*! No one did this to me. I am responsible for my own health and realizing my own limitations. I thought I had to do it! I did not realize until much later that I had taken on a burden that the Lord did not mean for me to carry. The church was His, not mine. He wanted me to roll that weight onto Him. It took a long time to get that through my determined mind! In the meantime, it affected my health. I simply did not realize how much! Stress is mean. It does not play fair. It seeks to conquer. And satan will pour it on if we do not shut it down.

When the people left that we were so close to – who were an integral part of the ongoing ministry – just seemed to be the last straw! It hurt our hearts. It didn't take long for satan to <u>use</u> the experience to war against my mind, to debilitate me, that it was all my fault, to minimize me, to silence me.

We had no answers to the questions of WHY or WHAT happened?? Communication seemed to be stymied.

The sense of rejection was overwhelming, and it was exhausting! Loyalty matters and we felt abandoned. The situation became worse for me because it became a spiritual issue. I felt like I had failed the Lord terribly and how would I ever recover from that? Why would He ever use me again? I had lost my perspective.

How does something like this happen? It happens when we get "out of balance" on trying to manage everything and everyone. This is a favorite tool of satan. It is subtle because he knows how much we love our family, our job, our ministry, our church, etc. He will then twist that against us and make it seem that it is up to US to work things out for everyone! Typically, things still can go wrong and everyone is unhappy, including us.

The loss of perspective was my greatest struggle. This was the aftermath of those who left. It was satan's way to rob me – if possible – of my future and my ministry but most importantly, my faith. It would only be a matter of time to see who would win out. I will go ahead and tell you now. It was not satan. There was still a valley for me to walk through before I reached my mountain. The Lord drew me aside for a season for healing and refreshing and restoration. The broken vessel was taken aside to allow the Potter his handiwork to mend it. I was unable to continue in ministry. We had to walk away from our vision. It was over.

This was earth shattering to me. The Lord called me to teach many years prior to this and that was my goal in life. I wanted to share His Word and let others know how good

He is, how great His love is for each of us in sending His Son to die for our sins. But now, I was weak physically from the demands *I allowed* to wear me down. I had to face the reality of where I was in life.

When we are facing a physical issue, it is much easier for satan to work against our mental and emotional and spiritual wellbeing. Issues tend to mushroom when you aren't well physically which can lead to a loss of perspective! You simply don't see things in the right way, you don't hear things the right way. I can honestly say, this spiritual attack was unlike anything I had ever experienced. *It was a setup* to bring a new list of problems for me. The saying that when you get knocked down, get right back up again works only in some cases. My "get up" was "long gone". I needed more than that to rise from this. And I would. But it would be the Lord's way and not through a cliché. I just wasn't there yet.

I spent about 6 months dealing with self-recrimination, regrets, and resentment. I wanted to let others know how hurt Terry and I both were. The Lord changed my heart on that. He spoke to me that I wasn't to defend myself. I was to handle things as Joseph did in the Bible. There were those who treated him so terribly. They mistreated him, belittled him, and went so far as to sell him into slavery to get him out of their lives! And this is done by his own brothers! Dysfunctional family well describes this one. People can stoop pretty low when they have enough hate and jealousy in their hearts. Evidently these brothers did.

Joseph's example was remarkable and applicable to our situation. It would have been understandable if Joseph had taken the matter into his own hands at the first opportunity and retaliated against those who had mistreated him so viciously. His new position in the Egyptian government certainly gave him that opportunity. Joseph made the better choice, however. Instead of taking the low road, he took the high one and made it possible for his brothers and their families to have food during a famine. Such an act of grace! Not retaliation.

Joseph learned the importance of having the right perspective! He didn't tell others how awful his brothers were. He didn't ask his boss to help him annihilate them. He stayed on course with what the Lord had given him to do and to be, even though he was not in the place he *wanted* to be. He came to understand, God had him right where he needed to be for His purpose that would unfold in the future. Jospeh's faith had to trust in the Sovereignty of God for both the immediate present and the future. Of course, the Lord turned it all to Joseph's good and the good of his people at just the right time.

Terry and I had to follow this example and not retaliate or tear others down to build ourselves up. To hold our peace when it feels justified to speak out takes a lot of grace! Fortunately, God willingly supplied it. There was more at stake than just our hurt feelings and disappointment. We would lose favor with the Lord if we mishandled the feelings of others or sought to harm the stature of others. That would be a no win situation.

I must say – it was not easy to follow in Joseph's footsteps. Doing the right thing is not always the easy thing to do! I don't have a problem standing up for myself but this was not the right approach for this matter. It did add to my angst, however. My hope was not lost but it was strained. My faith may have been weak but it was still there.

I knew for me to recover, my faith in God would be the only way it would happen. I would whisper my prayers to the Lord. I knew I still had to hold on to what the Scripture says about me so I would whisper the verses that I was holding onto. For instance, Psalm 118: 17 King David wrote "I shall not die, but live, and declare the works of the Lord." I did this every day. Sometimes more than once.

Terry would hold me and faithfully prayed for me through it all. We prayed for each other because he was disheartened as well. The Lord eventually revealed to him a vision of an old model car with a luggage rack with straps that was holding the luggage in place. When this happened, the Lord spoke to Terry's heart and asked him: "You see the car with the luggage strapped on?" Yes, he saw it all right. The Lord spoke to Terry's heart right then and there and told him that the car represented him carrying unnecessary baggage that was filled with hurt and disappointment from our painful experience. The Lord gave him these instructions: "cut those straps, let the baggage drop off and do not look back." In that very moment, as the Presence of the Lord ministered to him, he let it all go and he sensed in his spirit the release he had been longing for. He has never looked back. Nothing is worth holding onto if it is only dead weight, useless nonsense, or meaningless worries. And, yes, even disappointments or betrayals – all our losses that seem to block our moving forward in life! Our future will be forever changed when we let it all go.

I would recommend to any pastor or church leader or anyone in position is to pay attention to any "cracks" in the unity of your church or organization or even family. Seek to address it through prayer and wisdom and conversation. When unity is broken, things can crumble quickly. With sustained unity of purpose and vision, nothing can defeat you. Unfortunately, we did not have this opportunity.

If I could tell the world anything, I would tell them to trust in the God of the Bible, that it contains the truth that will set us free, that will make us whole, that points us to the Savior, the Lord Jesus Christ who is able to change our lives now and for eternity's sake. I needed an overhaul mentally, emotionally and spiritually. God's Word, His Spirit and His Name gave it to me. It was my answer.

Jesus is more real to me than I can ever convey to someone. He brought me to the place of surrender where I would let go of the disappointment, the hurt, even the anger and most of all the self-blame. It would be the decision that turned everything around.

"If I say, "My foot slips," Your mercy,
O Lord, will hold me up."
Psalm 94: 18

35

CHAPTER SEVEN

The First Step on My Path Forward

Terry and I are so grateful for the precious friends that He has given us that have lasted over 40 years. Several months after we closed the church, one of those friends, Rhonda Lee, called to see how I was doing. She could tell I wasn't doing well. We talked for a while and she told me that she and another close friend of ours, Vera Ferguson wanted to come visit me. I knew they would come and pray. I was so ready for that. We had prayed together many times for many needs through the years and the Lord gave us many answers! This day could be the same!

It didn't take long for Rhonda and Vera to arrive. They were a welcome sight! We had a good visit, and I was able to unload all the negative things that were crowding my heart. I was near rock bottom, thinking that God wouldn't use me anymore. They rejected that idea in no uncertain terms and encouraged me that the Lord still had plans for my life. They prayed for me and the Lord touched me. Then, Vera told me something I did not expect to hear. She said "Myra, you need to go to the people who hurt you and tell them you forgive them and ask that they forgive you." Not only that – she also told me that for me to get well, I needed to do this. I can tell you, I wasn't expecting that! Rhonda agreed with the loving and wise instruction Vera gave me. I struggled to get a grip on this idea. It may sound simple but it was not simplistic! It was a profound thing to contemplate and to execute.

I had prayed often for those who hurt us in those last few months. I believe I meant it. But now, for me to reach out to them and say that, seemed like a very hard thing for me to face. I had not seen them for several months, nor had I spoken with them. I did not think I could do it. This was no surprise to the Lord. He knew my heart had been broken. But He also knew the only medicine that would heal it. Forgiveness extended to an offender is stronger than the offense when it is done in sincerity. I knew that somehow God's strength would be waiting for me the moment I needed it.

The next morning, I knew in my heart, this was the day to follow the word that my friends had given me. Proverbs 27: 17 tells us "As iron sharpens iron, so a man sharpens the countenance of his friend." My precious friends came to me with the truth of Scripture to sharpen me, make me a better person, not a bitter one, to whittle away all the garbage that was built in my mind and crowding out my spirit.

It was a bold step to take but it was time. I wanted to be well *more than* I wanted to hold all this negative junk in my heart and mind. As I sat at our desk, I prayed – again. Yes, the Lord still wanted me to do this! But He never forces us to do the right thing. And there is reward when we do! To be sure: God cannot bless us beyond our last obedience. If we willfully disregard His direction, then that is open rebellion on our part, which is unacceptable. He has so much more to bless us with if we take the necessary steps to do things His way. I asked Him to give me the words to say. I wrote them down just in case I forgot them! Now, I needed my heart to stop pounding so hard! I had two calls to make.

Thankfully, all parties were at home and we all spoke in peace. They were happy that I called. I was able to convey the reason for my call. I stated that we didn't understand why they left the church and us, but I wanted to express my forgiveness of them for the hurt that it caused. I apologized for any hurt I caused them. I told them I was doing this because I wanted to be well more than I wanted to hold on to the hurt. They received my words and my forgiveness. It was time for us all to move forward with the Lord. There was still peace and joy among us when we hung up the phone. Thank you, Lord Jesus.

It is an amazing thing that God does for us when we follow through in doing the *"right thing"*. He steps in and gives us the extra measure of grace in which to do it! Joy filled my heart as I walked through our home! I realize this may seem like just a simple thing to have done! What is the big deal? I will have to ask you to accept my word on it. It was not a simple thing. Otherwise, the whole world would be at peace with one another! My future depended on taking the steps that I did. It has been more than worth it. It felt awfully good to be saved, to know that I was His, that He didn't give up on me, nor would He!

It had only been a matter of time for me to get to the place where I was surrendered to the Potter and His reforming me to be more useful in the future. The door had opened for healing to flow into my life.

The very opposite is true if we resist the leading of the Holy Spirit to do the right thing in any given situation. Holding on to negative, detrimental attitudes, especially unforgiveness will never affect the offender. The offended will find themselves in a deep spiritual hole that is very hard to climb out of. If we will swallow our pride and take the step forward that is both liberating and healing, we will see dramatic changes take place.

"A friend loves at all times, and a brother is born for adversity." Proverbs 17: 17

CHAPTER EIGHT

Times of Refreshing

The Lord has amazing timing. He knows exactly when to bring people into our lives, and He knows exactly when to move them on. It is important that we realize when He is at work and not try to do it ourselves, either coming or going. I had to learn that there are people who come into our lives to stay but there are also those who come for a season only. The Lord helped us to not grieve over what could have been but to move on in faith as we regained our footing. We came to understand and accept that we should not return to pastoring. The Lord graciously taught us that He allows us to do certain things, to test our wings so that we discover that is NOT His perfect will for us. We did not argue.

He led us to return to the church we were members in the early years of our marriage, Mount Paran Church in Atlanta, Georgia. It was a drive now for us, but it was just what the Doctor ordered. From the first Sunday we were back, it was like heaven opening up with refreshing and renewal poured into our hearts and minds. In each service the music and songs and sermon were tailored just for us! I mean that sincerely. The Lord directed our steps to be there at just the right time and for the right purpose.

Eventually, the Lord opened the door for me to teach again. While it didn't happen overnight, it did happen at just the right time: when the Potter determined the vessel to be ready. I served there for seven wonderful years until the Lord directed us to find a church closer to home. It was time.

There are times in life that you have to just say "the Lord orchestrated this!" Such was the case one hot Saturday in August. We were invited to a birthday party and we were completely surprised when we saw old friends from Mount Holly! Terry and I had discussed where we wanted to visit that Sunday and of course, Mount Holly was at the top of the list to consider. We had a wonderful chat with our friends, and they caught us up on things happening there. They told us that Pastor Guyton was retiring and that Jeff Maxell would be the new lead Pastor. We have known Pastor Jeff and his wife, Stephanie and their children, Bethany and Cameron, since they were born. That was over 20 years ago. We were confident that the church would thrive under his leadership and their joint ministry. After seeing these dear friends and talking with them was not incidental. It was the Lord confirming to our hearts that He wanted us to return to MHC.

The next morning we walked into Mount Holly Church, Carrollton, Georgia and it was truly wonderful. It was like we never left. It was so wonderful to see other cherished friends again. The Lord had us at the right place at the right time because that summer, Terry had an injury working on our deck stairs. It was awful and scary. For several months we were seeing different doctors and specialists, getting this test, that MRI, this CT Scan. Pastor Jeff and members of the flock prayed earnestly for him. It was tremendous to have someone who is available to you to pray and care about you when you are going through challenging circumstances. Pastor Jeff does that for all his congregation. He is a very accomplished preacher as well. Mount Holly is so blessed to have him and his family. This meant a lot to us as we faced this tough place with Terry's health. It was difficult to see someone you love and cherish be in pain and anguish. But God had a plan in place to change all that. He touched Terry and healed him and he is back being the busy man he always has been. To God be the glory.

Since our return to MHC, the Lord opened the door for us to begin a class again on Sunday mornings. It has been so marvelous to have such a class with beautiful hearts that love to study the Scriptures. I suppose you could say the Lord had the last word on our being used in ministry again! He said YES!

And we are very thankful He did! He brought us full circle. No one should ever count a child of God out! God alone determines that!

You have turned for me my mourning into dancing; You have put off my sackcloth and clothed me with gladness; to the end that my glory (my soul) may sing praise to You and not be silent, O Lord my God, I will give thanks to You forever."
Psalm 30: 11-12

STAY THE COURSE: THE PATH OF FAITH, WISDOM, AND PEACE
With each step – We move forward

Everyone has a story. Mine pales in comparison to those who have endured broken hearts and broken lives through no fault of their own. Still, our story has merit and is worthy of consideration. The Lord proved Himself more faithful than we ever experienced before. He was long suffering in teaching us valuable lessons that will last a lifetime. Lessons we hope we never have to repeat!

In closing I would like to share some of the truths that the Lord blessed us to gain. They are truths that will benefit anyone who has been wounded, pushed to the breaking point, feel rejected, or you find yourself struggling to rise above the pain of defeat and humiliation. You may be a person of faith in God or perhaps you aren't. Please know that the truth I have written here can benefit you if you will open your heart to it.

1. There are probably more books written on prayer than anything. Prayer is about building a relationship with Him which is made possible through His Son, Jesus Christ. God has given us this wonderful opportunity to speak with Him anytime, any day. We do not have to talk like anyone else

does. He only wants us to speak from our heart. In fact, Psalm 62: 8 tells us "Trust in Him at all times, you people; pour out your heart before Him; God is a refuge for us." At all times, it says. He is always ready to listen to the cry of our heart.

Having close communication with the Lord keeps us well-grounded and in fellowship with Him. It is important that we not let any person, place or thing hinder our prayer life by always making time for prayer and reading Scripture. Making requests of Him is His delight. He welcomes us to His throne to do so. The Lord may send answers that are different than our requests. They are *better*. His timing is perfect and is worth waiting for.

2. Respect the sovereignty of God. He is in control, not you, not me. It may look like man or woman is at times, but they are deceived if they think that. God is sovereign and will move anything or anyone that might not be His choice for our lives at this time. Let it be. Let it go. He always has our best interests at heart.

3. Choose faith, not fear, not worry. Faith can move mountains and fear only makes them appear bigger. They aren't bigger than God. Nothing and no one are. Faith in God can change any circumstance for our good because we trust Him and live for Him. Worry will only change us into warts. That is not a good look. There will always be things out of our control. This is no surprise to God. He is on top of things.

4. People are people. We must accept that and not try to mold others into what we want them to be. Live free of the need to change others. That is God's department alone. He isn't hiring assistants. I know. I tried more than once…He still said no. Time to move on!

5. Recognize your weaknesses and your strengths. Don't let others pull your chain either way. Establish your personal boundaries and stick to them. You and I aren't the answer for everything and everyone. Saying no *as needed* isn't just an option. It is an answer you can live with.

6. Don't do life all on your own. Have a safety net of close friends or family *that you know* are faithful and that have your best interests at heart. You can talk things out with them and be confident it will remain confidential. The best friends are those who love us when we are wrong and they tell us when we are wrong and they hang around to pray for us to get beyond it. They are priceless and so is their wise counsel.

7. Failure is the largest classroom there is. AND it is always full because we all have a lot more to learn and our mistakes teach us the most. Let us use our time there wisely. Failure isn't final unless we choose to believe in it more than the Grace of God to help us get beyond it. Choose Grace. Speak Grace. Live Grace.

8. Don't waste your sorrows or your tears or your time over the past. Nothing is changed by looking backward. Everything in life grows – as long as it is alive! If you are alive – then

you have the potential to grow as a human being in spite of your own faults and failures as the rest of us. Mistakes that we learn from are meant to make us better, not to grieve over.

9. We all understand there is a spiritual enemy that is at work in the world. He seeks to run roughshod over people's lives with torment and degradation. Hit that reject button! Stand your ground spiritually and speak the Word of God over your life and renounce him and his activities in Jesus Name. When we submit ourselves to God, the enemy has to flee. (James 4: 7)   Don't worry about him. Stand in faith in what you know God's Word says about you.

10. Perhaps the number one obstacle we human beings face is the need to understand the *why* of every circumstance we experience! I can't tell you how many times I have asked that of the Lord. So far, He has not revealed a single reason of *why*. You would think I would be beyond that by now but….maybe one day. I have at least progressed to stopping myself and remind myself that the why of anything is God's department and He alone has the key to get in.

What He has helped me to do, is get control of my thoughts of needing to know all the answers and instead – keep walking The Path Forward one step at a time by faith in Him, in His goodness and in His great love for Terry and me and for all those who love Him. Proverbs 3: 5-6 tells me how to do this: "Trust in the Lord with all your heart, and lean not on your own understanding; In all your ways acknowledge Him, and He shall direct your paths." These paths ALWAYS move forward! Find yours with God's help.

11. It is an unfortunate and sad truth – there are those who try to take advantage of others, to use others. It can tear our heart out, if we aren't careful. It can bring up very negative responses from us, such as retaliation.

It is understandable but that can only bring more angst into our lives. There is an answer for it that is totally opposite of revenge. That would be to pray for the person that does this. It may be an excruciating thought to do that when our heart is broken but by praying for them, we release all that hostility and disappointment – and especially the pain – to the one and only person that can change anything and anyone. That would be the Lord.

When we pray in this way, we place circumstances – and the people involved – at the feet of Jesus to work in their hearts and lives and confront their behavior, we are giving up the need and the right to be the one that punishes our offender. Punishment isn't ours to mete out. It only belongs to God. (Romans 12:19)

Anger, unforgiveness, and resentment are hard taskmasters. Fire them and move on. Live free of that garbage. Don't take all these negatives *into your future* by hanging on to them. It will not change anything! But, releasing it from our heart will change us every time. And for the better!

12. The Lord Jesus came to give us His joy and that we might have it to the full. (John 15: 11) His joy in the worst of times, the darkest of times, the loneliest of times. This is only possible as we live a life of trust in His goodness that far outweighs the awful circumstance we may be living through.

Joy isn't about skipping down the road or ignoring the severity of a crisis. Joy is something much deeper within us. It is that sense of knowing that our God is in control of things, that we can take our hands off the wheel of our life and trust Him to get us where we need to be safely. And joy is being assured He is with us regardless of how things look or feel.

Life is SHORT. We not only live it one day at a time, one hour at a time, one minute at a time. This moment – right now – is all we have. How full would our lives be if we lived it in as much joy as possible. When we *choose* joy our journey is a lot sweeter.

> "These things I have spoken to you, that in Me you may
> have peace. In the world you will have tribulation;
> but be of good cheer, I have overcome the world."
> *John 16: 33*

EPILOGUE

Let me share with you one of the most powerful verses in the Bible. If we live by this one, our lives will be dramatically changed for the better. Here it is.

> *"And now abide faith, hope, love, these three; but the greatest is love." I Corinthians 13: 13*

Faith in God is the most powerful concept on earth. It has the capacity to change circumstances that are beyond our control. Faith is not complicated. It is our belief system based on the Word of God that is changeless because its Author is. Faith may be strong one day and a little feeble another day. Encourage yourself in the Lord and that faith will begin to rise up and ready to take on the next giant!

Hope is what inspires us. It helps us get up in the morning with anticipation for a better day. The reason being that our hope is rooted in the truth of God's Word. It is the confident expectation we have simply because we can stand on the Promises of God for our lives and can depend on His faithfulness.

Love…God's love should be our motivation for each day. It is expressed by letting others know that they matter, that we care, that we are willing to help them at their point of need – with wise boundaries. God's love equals kindness. That is a clear indicator that our world is in need of a baptism of God's love since there is so much hate instead. Love is obvious when it doesn't find fault, it covers it. It doesn't assess blame, it forgives it. It isn't prideful, it is humble. It is patient, it is forbearing. No wonder it is the greatest.

> May your Faith in God remain strong, His peace
> to be your guide, your cup of joy to be full,
> and that His love be your comfort.

REMEMBER

I have shared with you my testimony of the goodness of God at work in the lives of two people who love Him with all their heart. I hope it has ministered to you. God is bigger than any hurt that you have experienced in your life. I want you to remember that His goodness has nothing to do with the circumstances you face in this life. The Lord's love never fades. Circumstances come and go just as people may, but His love is permanent. Whatever your circumstances, whatever area of brokenness you may have in your life, whatever burdens you have today, remember that He cares for you. He is only a prayer away. He can change circumstances and people. He can heal brokenness and lift heavy burdens.

If you do not know the reality of your sins being forgiven and being assured of going to heaven after this life is passed, please call on the Lord today. Simply ask Him to forgive you and commit your life to Him. Study His Word and live by it and your life will have a peace and joy that you never dreamed possible. A new season awaits you in Christ!

ENDORSEMENTS

"In her new book, Myra Woodbridge, whom I have known for many years, offers a heartfelt and personal testimony of faith through life's difficult trials. "The Path Forward" is a must-read for anyone seeking hope, comfort, guidance, and a deeper understanding of God's unwavering presence in our lives. It is a powerful reminder that with God, no challenge is insurmountable, and no situation is helpless."

– Jeff Maxwell
Lead Pastor, Mount Holly Church,
Carrollton, Georgia

"Myra's book is a testament to her gift and anointing as a teacher. Her insights inspire and transform, making complex ideas accessible and profound. A must-read for anyone seeking wisdom and guidance."

– Pat Dominguez

"I have known Myra Woodbridge since the mid 90's. She follows the Holy Spirit's leading in her teaching of the Word of God. Her teaching inspires me to dig deeper in the Word and in my relationship with Christ. Her devotion to the Lord and her teaching inspires so many, she is a blessing!

– Karen West

"Myra is an inspiration to me and I am sure she will be to you as well."

– Connie Reece

"Myra's spiritual gifts are many, but her ability to help readers look past life's challenges and disappointments, which are something we all are subject to face, to see the lavish blessings of God's healing is remarkable. She is an anointed communicator. She courageously shares the gospel of Jesus through her writing and her teaching."

– Leesa Copeland

"I attended the first class Terry and Myra led at Mount Holly Church. It is an answer to prayer that they are back with us and leading a Sunday morning class again. The teaching on Prayer that she taught has greatly impacted my life and the way that I pray. I love her teachings."

– Irma Wilkison

"Myra has the ability to bring the Word of God to practical applications for life. Myra's teaching is Scripture based straight from the Word and is very encouraging to all who have heard her teach."

– Jack West

"Terry and Myra have been a blessing to me dating back to the first class they led at Mount Holly Church. I enjoy your teaching of God's Word. May the Lord keep you both always."

– Barbara Birge

"My dad always said if you find a good Sunday School teacher, you had better hang on to her. Terry and Myra led a class at Mount Holly several years ago now and we are glad to have them leading a new class now at MHC. Myra is a great teacher and she and Terry are always there for me when I need them to pray. I look forward to hearing her every Sunday. They both are a blessing to us all."

– Pat Carden

ABOUT THE AUTHOR

Myra's teaching ministry spans over four decades, and her dedication to sharing the profound truths of Scripture shines through in every facet of her work. At Mount Holly Church in Carrollton, Ga., she and her husband, Terry, lead a vibrant Bible Study that delves deep into the historical and linguistic context of biblical texts, offering insightful life applications along the way.

With a rich background that includes a radio ministry, television interviews, and speaking engagements at conferences, Myra brings a wealth of experience to her teachings. Her debut book, "Chosen of the Lord – Broken in Heart," published in 2008, reflects her profound understanding of biblical principles intertwined with real-life experiences.

What sets Myra apart is her commitment to rigorous study under the guidance of renowned Bible scholars like Dr. Paul L. Walker, Dr. M.G. McLuhan, and Dr. David Cooper. Their influence has not only shaped her theological insights but also fueled her passion for serving the Lord and impacting lives positively through the transformative power of Scripture.

Myra's topical Bible Studies are a testament to her balanced approach, weaving together historical context, linguistic nuances, and practical wisdom to help others connect deeply with God's Word. She firmly believes that the Scriptures hold the keys to unlocking a life of purpose, fulfillment, and spiritual growth, and her ministry reflects this unwavering conviction.

www.ingramcontent.com/pod-product-compliance
Lightning Source LLC
Chambersburg PA
CBHW050904120626
46554CB00003B/1008